This life is indeed a journey. So often we become entirely focused on getting to where we want to be and arriving at some pinnacle of achievement that we abandon the joy of simply living and learning in our everyday lives. I challenge you to stop right now and just enjoy the moment. Look at the blessing of who you are and what you have and offer praise to God for this precious gift of life. I pray that this book enhances your understanding of faith and how it operates to further God's divine purpose in your life. It is for those who have an ear to hear, those who are sincerely ready to offer obedience, and those who have resigned every manipulation and scheme at the feet of our King Jesus.

Mary

Faith

Confessions

for

The Journey

Faith Confessions for The Journey

Published by Eve of Destiny Publishing

PO Box 681084

Franklin, TN 37068

www.marytiller.com

Unless otherwise noted, all Scripture quotations are from the King James Version of the Bible.

ISBN 978-0-6151-6215-7

Printed in the United States of America

Dedication

This book is dedicated to my husband. Who has provided a foundation of love and support for me to be able to flourish in the gifts that God has given me and has been a constant force of faith in my life. Larry, you have been my champion, and my very best friend. I have never seen God's face, but I am certain that you look like him. You are such a kind man full of His goodness, I love you deeply and these words just aren't enough.

TABLE OF CONTENTS

INTRODUCTION

Faith confessions serve two purposes, to identify the word of God, and to practice hearing it over and over again. I pray that as I share some of the faith confessions I have written over the years that you will be inspired to develop your own so that you can know, confess, and believe the will of God in your life, and see it come to pass. You will learn how to write a faith confession, and hear personal testimonies as well as scriptures to plant seeds of faith in your heart so that you can walk in your complete purpose and destiny in the Kingdom of God.

"So then faith cometh by hearing, and hearing by the word of God." Ro 10:17

So faith comes by hearing, and hearing, and then hearing some more. But if that was all there was to it, we could just go around all day repeating "I think I can, I think I can", or "I love myself", or saying a whole slew of rather catchy "new age", "quick fix", "what's wrong with me and why can't I get it together" phrases and be done with it. If hearing alone is all it takes then what about when people say things that are not true in your hearing. Such as, "You'll never amount to anything, or "You can't do it", or "You are just like your (fill in the blank)". Aren't you glad that faith is not just a matter of hearing? Here's the clincher! Are you ready? "Hearing comes by the word of God". That's it, the big finale, the punch line, and the mandatory ingredient to produce faith. If what you're hearing is not the word of God it does not and will not produce faith, not even a little bit. (Somebody is getting a life changing revelation on that statement alone) Hearing the kinds of things we just mentioned that are not based on the word of God can produce fear and bondage if we give way to them, but it will not produce faith! Why is that significant? Because God honors faith, he cosigns with faith and agrees with it because ultimately when we walk in faith, we are agreeing with God's word! Who in their right mind would not agree with themselves! God does not agree with "You'll never amount to anything, or "You can't do it", or "You are just like your (fill in the blank)". He agrees with, "I am more than a conqueror through Him that loved me, I can do all things through Christ that strengthens me, and I am fearfully and wonderfully made!"

If we understand the true character and integrity of God, then we know that God is good. His intentions are good, and His thoughts toward us are good. (Jer 29:11) The enemy is constantly trying to pervert our perception of God and cause us to question these cornerstones of God's character. For the record there is no evil in Him and no fault to find.

"Now faith is the substance of things hoped for, the evidence of things not seen." Heb 11:1

Relying on the bible for our definition of faith we conclude "Faith" is defined as the substance of things hoped for, the evidence of things not seen. So in essence we're talking substance, and evidence, not opinions or hearsay. Let's take a brief look at the words **substance** and **evidence** so that we can further our understanding.

"Substance" in this scripture comes from the Hebrew word "*Hupostasis*" and means a setting or placing under. In other words the substance is the very real structure or foundation that firmly supports the hope.

When it comes to evidence, we've all seen enough trials depicted on television or in living color to know the importance of evidence, and how without it there is no case. The Hebrew word is "*Elegchos*" and it means the proof by which a thing is proved or tested.

Those 2 scriptures tell us what faith is and how it comes…If we marry them it reads like this;

"Now the foundation of things hoped for and the proof of things not seen comes by hearing and that hearing comes by the word of God"

There is no way around it, you must hear the word of God to have faith, and you must have faith to please God (*Heb 11:6*). The Bible instructs us that we will have what we say. I cannot tell you how often I heard this spoken until I finally began to believe and practice it. !!!!!!!!This book will provide examples, and instructions on how you can practice hearing the word of God as it relates uniquely to your life in the form of a faith confession.

"For as the body without the spirit is dead, so faith without works is dead also." Jas 2:26

You can see for yourself what the scripture is telling us. Simply stated, hearing the word of God produces faith, that faith is activated when you match it with your works otherwise it is dead. If you hear the word and believe it, your works will demonstrate that belief.

"What then am I supposed to do?" you might ask. Well, each situation is different and requires your obedience to the "right now" voice of God. What carried a breakthrough for me may not have the same result for you. God will lead you as you pray and seek His wisdom and direction.

Sometimes an attitude and disposition may have to change. Other times there may be a specific course of action that you are instructed to take by God in your prayer time or through a true prophet.

I know for certain that when we demonstrate our living faith to God, it pleases Him. Then He comes alongside of it and says, "according to your faith be it unto you" *Mt 9:29*

I will share this example from scripture with you (read Joshua chapter 1) because it demonstrates this point perfectly.

After having wandered in the wilderness for forty years, Joshua heard the word of the Lord concerning Israel possessing the land of Canaan. Now, if it were me, I am not sure if I would still have hope after all that time. But Joshua heard the word and it produced faith in him. Then he confessed what he had heard and told the children of Israel that they were going to cross over the Jordan to possess the land in three days. Talk about a faith confession! He literally said, "Hey we are doing this in three days, so get ready! And the people said, "Yeah the Lord is with you like He was with Moses, and anybody that doesn't agree with Joshua we are going to kill them". Joshua acting on the word he heard and believed sent out spies and they came back with a much different report than the crew Moses had sent 40 years before. This time they said, "Yup Joshua, God gave us this land, and even the people that live in the land know He gave it to us because they are afraid of us!" Let me say that I believe when Joshua confessed the word of the Lord it went from his mouth out into the atmosphere and resulted in a sound carried on the wings of the wind and not only did the people that were with him hear it and believe, but it traveled to their enemy's camp and they believed also. That is the power of a faith confession!

You will remember that that when the children of Israel crossed a sea with Moses, God had given Moses the instruction to stick out his rod. As a result, the sea parted and everyone crossed over on dry ground. This time if you can picture it, there are thousands if not millions of people following behind the priest who are carrying the arc of the covenant. God does not instruct Joshua to stretch out a rod as He did Moses and have the Jordan part then tell them to cross, which would have been nice because the bible says that this was the season of harvest so the Jordan was overflowing on all its banks. Instead, He tells him that when the priest feet come to the brink of the water that they will stand still in the Jordan. In other words, "you should trust Me by now so go on and get in, show Me your faith" So they do as instructed (obedience) and the priests dip their feet in the brim of the water (their faith at work) and the bible says that the waters rose up in a heap and all the people of Israel crossed over on dry ground. Hallelujah!

See it is not just enough to know the word of God, you must hear it, confess it, obey it, and then demonstrate the works of it! Let's get started.

CHAPTER 1

Getting Personal

I am going to share my "Personal Faith Confession" with you. It is the first faith confession I ever wrote. After being introduced to the truth about faith and God's word it was something I set my mind to do. I began by making a list of issues that I wanted to address in my life, and then researched scriptures related to each and every issue. For example, I wanted my character to represent Christ and for people to see Him in me. So it was obvious that I needed the fruits of the spirit to become fully operational. Let's just say maybe 2 or 3 were working okay, but I had some real challenges with some of them like "patience". (I thought I heard an Amen out there) Incorporating this in my confession not only resulted in me being reminded everyday, but over time God began to prune me so that I could bring forth good fruit. If I am being honest I can say that he is still pruning.

Another good example is the portion of my confession dedicated to the music ministry. I understood that from my study of II Chronicles 20 that there are 3 main spirits that attack music ministry. These are pride, jealousy, and sexual sin. You will find that people with a powerful music ministry will have to combat these spirits in one form or another at some point in their ministry. Upon realizing that God had anointed me for this ministry I knew that I would not be an exception and made sure to include this in my confession so that I might begin to avoid some unnecessary battles.

Whatever is important to you in your personal life, you too can study the word of God and find His will so that you can begin to exercise faith and see those things come to pass. I should bring your attention to the fact that my confession is not akin to a list for Santa Claus. The issues that are addressed are directly related to my revealed purpose in the kingdom and my maturity as a believer in Jesus Christ. There are no cars, houses, clothes etc. addressed here. The bible is clear that if we seek first the kingdom of heaven these things will be added. So be careful to examine your motives.

Personal Faith Confession

Father I am Your daughter, and I love Your name Jesus. I thank You for Your mercy and I abound in Your grace. I thank You for making Your name great in and through my life.

I commit this day for the purpose of ministry. I thank You that You have strengthened my hands for the work. I am being lost in Your anointing, so that my actions, my behavior, and my demeanor reflect positively on the kingdom of heaven. I thank You that I am patient with others and sensitive to their needs. My life produces evidence of the fruits of the spirit. In Your name, Love, Joy, Peace, Temperance, Patience, Meekness, Faith, and Gentleness are growing out of me.

Thank You Lord that the anointing of chief musician and psalmist are upon me. I praise You that I am hearing new and fresh melodies from the gates of heaven that could only come from You. Father, I love to worship You and sing praises in Your presence. I thank You that You have chosen me to lead Your people in worship and given me the ministry of song. In Jesus name the spirits of pride, jealousy, and sexual sin are confused and taken captive by my own praises and the praises of Your people that they may perpetually and consistently receive a life changing revelation of You, through Your word, by Your spirit, and under Your anointing.

Thank You Jesus for leading and guiding me. I thank You that the choices and decisions I make are submerged in Your will for my life. I thank You for the supernatural favor towards me. I thank You that You are putting me on the minds and hearts of people that I may not even know, and that they are being motivated by Your spirit to intercede on my behalf. I thank You that every song and every note I sing and that is recorded is inspired by You, and serves to bring glory to You name alone, Jesus.

Lord, I honor You with the first fruits in all that I have and all that I do. I thank You that the principle of first fruits is operational in my life. I thank You that as I give, seeds are planted, and fruit is multiplied back to me to be prosperous and have a super abundance that I may give more and produce more for the uplifting of Your kingdom.

Father I give You the first of my love, the first of my talent, the first of my time, and it is all multiplied back to me in super abundance. I thank You that I am an excellent steward over Your money, and You can trust me. I praise You that as I apply the wisdom You have given by Your word with the guidance of Your spirit unnecessary financial debt is eliminated and I am financially liberated in Jesus name.

My body is Your temple and You dwell in me. I thank You that I do not have the desire to overeat, in Your name Jesus. I thank You for guiding me in my choices of food and the amounts to consume supernaturally by Your anointing. I rebuke un-Godly cravings in the name of Jesus. By Your grace I exercise daily and my metabolism is increased. I am anointed to eat right and be healthy. By Your spirit, unnecessary fat is being burned away from my body, In Jesus name.

Lord, I delight in You, and I love being with You. It is easy for me to rejoice with others because I know I have not been forgotten. I thank You for my wonderful, Godly husband. I praise You that he is Your best. I thank You Lord that I am being prepared and made ready for marriage, even in his absence. I believe that he is being manifested in Your perfect time, and that every event and circumstance is being orchestrated for the purpose of joining us together to have dominion. Father I cast down every imagination in Jesus name. I praise You for no delays only perfect time.

I love You Lord. Teach me today. I am Your sheep and I know Your voice, another I will not follow. Reveal the mysteries of Your word, change me, and renew my mind. Be with me today as You are on all days. In Jesus name, I confess and believe.

Ga 4:7

Now you are no longer a slave but God's own child. And since you are his child, everything he has belongs to you

Ga 3:29

And if ye be Christ's, then are ye Abraham's seed, and heirs according to the promise.

Ge 12:2

And I will make of thee a great nation, and I will bless thee, and make thy name great; and thou shalt be a blessing:

Ne 2:18

Then I told them of the hand of my God which was good upon me; as also the king's words that he had spoken unto me. And they said, Let us rise up and build. So they strengthened their hands for this good work.

Ga 5:22-23

But the fruit of the Spirit is love, joy, peace, longsuffering, gentleness, goodness, faith, Meekness, temperance: against such there is no law.

2Sa 23:1

Now these be the last words of David. David the son of Jesse said, and the man who was raised up on high, the anointed of the God of Jacob, and the sweet psalmist of Israel, said,

1Sa 16:23

And it came to pass, when the evil spirit from God was upon Saul, that David took an harp, and played with his hand: so Saul was refreshed, and was well, and the evil spirit departed from him.

2Ch 20:21 -22

And when he had consulted with the people, he appointed singers unto the LORD, and that should praise the beauty of holiness, as they went out before the army, and to say, Praise the LORD; for his mercy endureth forever And when they began to sing and to praise, the LORD set ambushments against the children of Ammon, Moab, and mount Seir, which were come against Judah; and they were smitten

Pr 3:6

> In all thy ways acknowledge him, and he shall direct thy paths.

Pr 3:9

> Honour the LORD with thy substance, and with the firstfruits of all thine increase:

1Co 6:19

> What? know ye not that your body is the temple of the Holy Ghost which is in you, which ye have of God, and ye are not your own?

Ps 37:4

> Delight thyself also in the LORD; and he shall give thee the desires of thine heart.

2Co 10:5

> Casting down imaginations, and every high thing that exalteth itself against the knowledge of God, and bringing into captivity every thought to the obedience of Christ;

Lu 8:10

> And he said, Unto you it is given to know the mysteries of the kingdom of God: but to others in parables; that seeing they might not see, and hearing they might not understand.

1 Co 4:1

> Let a man so account of us, as of the ministers of Christ, and stewards of the mysteries of God

Job 10:27

> My sheep hear my voice, and I know them, and they follow me:

Mt 10:16

> Behold, I send you forth as sheep in the midst of wolves: be ye therefore wise as serpents and harmless as doves.

Your Personal Faith Confession

List each issue you wish to address.	Now list the scriptures you found related to each issue. (Strong's Exhaustive Concordance is a great resource)
1.	
2.	
3.	
4.	
5.	

Now in your own words get started on your personal faith confession based on the scriptures you have found.

_____

_____

_____

_____

_____

_____

_____

_____

_____

_____

_____

CHAPTER 2

Getting Down to Business

You will notice that although I base my confession on scriptures, you can definitely hear my own voice rather clearly. It is great to memorize scriptures and believe me they will pop up in your spirit just when you need them. However, your faith confession should not read as if it were a lost gospel. Be real with God, He knows us very well and He is not impressed by us simply memorizing scripture or using impressively complex words. Keep it simple, and keep it real.

I firmly believe that we are to be the head and not the tail. I believe it because the scripture says so. As sure as I am standing there are many of you reading this with dreams of business and enterprise. Sadly, some of us have bought into the whole, "It will never happen for me" movement (or should I say non-movement) and are sitting by while the faith filled believers open up shop. My brother and my sister I encourage you to get busy. There is a move of God going on and the thing He put in you is essential to your purpose in the Kingdom. It is a great big production, and we need you in your right place because it just doesn't work right without you.

God was talking to me about His Kingdom one day and He showed me a great big marching band on a football field. I was in the band and being given instructions to move here and go this way and that. Naturally, I was just concentrating on my part, making sure to get it right. Then I wasn't in the band anymore, I was in front of the band and I could see all the different members moving and began to realize there was a formation to this march, an actual plan. Then I was elevated to the top of the bleachers and I could see it all. Each band member's instrument not only made the melody of a great song, but each movement was perfectly choreographed making the most elegant production.

God spoke to me there and said, "This is My Kingdom". When we begin to realize that we are all a part of whole big production and that other people are relying on your obedience to the plan of God it makes you that much more committed to do whatever it takes to learn you part and be in your God given place. Some of us are to operate as entrepreneurs, and we can't be afraid to step out there and do it. Listen, the anointing and the grace of God is upon you to do His will. You better get ready; I can hear your part coming up!

A little sidebar for those of us with dreams and seemingly no resources, what do you really have to work with? For those who say you have nothing, I would admonish you to check again.

In II Kings 4 Elijah is confronted by a widow of a prophet. She is asking him what she is supposed to do to support herself and her two sons. She tells Elijah that her creditors are threatening to enslave her sons. In response, Elijah asks her what she has in her house. She replies that she has nothing but a pot of oil. Elijah then tells her to go and borrow vessels from her neighbors (this lady knew her neighbors, do you?), and says to make sure she gets more than a few. After borrowing the vessels she is instructed to shut herself and her sons in the house and pour the oil into the vessels filling them up. The bible says there was oil enough to fill every single vessel she had, and the oil only stopped when she ran out of vessels. The woman went back to Elijah and he told her to sell the oil, pay her debts, and live on the rest.

I am certain that after the oil was sold and the funds were counted, it probably crossed the widow's mind that if she had borrowed even more vessels, she would have had more oil to sell, and even more to live on.

I am speaking to believers who are faithful with the tithe and offering. There is oil that God wants to get to you, but you have not provided vessels. What are vessels you say? And why can't God just send me the check? Let me answer those questions for you.

Vessels are those business ideas and opportunities that keep coming to mind. Remember God is not in the business of hustling or causing folks to prosper at the expense of others so the ideas he gives provide service, benefit, and are full of integrity. You know, the ones you say are too hard or will take too much of the time that you don't have because you are too busy punching the clock! (I am not advising anyone to quit his or her job) Many times the ideas or instructions we receive will involve other people, and we just don't want to be bothered with having to borrow vessels from our neighbors. Or we think we have to know how it is all going to come together before we can get started. The widow woman did not know how the oil was going to meet her need until she went back to Elijah and he told her what to do. Sometimes you just have to move under the anointing and obey the prophetic voice of God! I find that we will give tithes and offerings and sew seed all over the place. But when it comes time to reaping we tend to show up at the harvest with no tools. I am not a farmer but I can just imagine a farmer trying to reap his cornfield without something to hold the corn. He would only be able to reap what he could hold. That same principle is at work in our lives. You ever wonder why every now and then you get a little bit here and a little bit there? It is because there is no room, no avenue, no vessel, nothing opened to receive and you are only able to walk away with what you can hold.

Well, why can't God just send me a check? Well my brothers and sisters He already has. It was sent over 2,000 years ago and was used to purchase your salvation! I am not saying that a check you were not expecting will not show up at your house every now and again. It happens all the time. But I admonish you to use the energy it takes to go to the mailbox and look for the unexpected check to stop at your neighbor's house and borrow a vessel!

Come on now, begin to see yourself the way God sees you in the production. You are important, you are valuable, and you are capable!

Entrepreneur

Father I am Your daughter and I love Your name Jesus. I thank You that You have caused me to be the head and not the tail. I thank You that it is Your will for me to prosper and have good success.

Lord I thank You that there is an entrepreneurial anointing on me and I am being led by Your spirit to make good sound business decisions. I thank You that I am blessed in business and return a hundred fold. Father I thank You that You are supernaturally giving me favor with lenders, grantors, and investors for capital. I thank You for perfecting the design and blueprints of my business and putting me in right relationships and partnerships according to Your will. I praise Your name that the information and skills that I have gathered throughout my career has prepared me with wisdom and knowledge and given me an appreciation and compassion for the people that work for and with me.

Father, I thank You that I am a generous and reasonable employer. I thank You Lord that my employees are blessed and enhanced by their employ. I thank You that their needs are met, and they do not lack healthcare insurance, homes, automobiles, food, and the things they desire. Lord I appreciate the people that You have entrusted to me and I thank You that they come to a closer relationship with You and their families see the fruit of their labor.

Lord I bless Your name for my desire to learn. I thank You that I am gaining useful information and insight that will assist in being thorough and concise as I build the business I know You desire for me to have. I thank You that it is easy for me to retain knowledge and I am not discouraged or overwhelmed by the enormous amount there is to learn. Father You know all things, I thank You for teaching me.

Father I thank You that my ministry, my marriage, and my business all work together to achieve the purpose for which I am uniquely created resulting in bringing glory and honor to Your name. In Your name I confess and believe.

De 28:13

And the LORD shall make thee the head, and not the tail; and thou shalt be above only, and thou shalt not be beneath; if that thou hearken unto the commandments of the LORD thy God, which I command thee this day, to observe and to do them:

Jos 1:8

This book of the law shall not depart out of thy mouth; but thou shalt meditate therein day and night, that thou mayest observe to do according to all that is written therein: for then thou shalt make thy way prosperous, and then thou shalt have good success.

Mr 4:20

And these are they which are sown on good ground; such as hear the word, and receive it, and bring forth fruit, some thirtyfold, some sixty, and some an hundred.

1Co 9:18-19

What is my reward then? Verily that, when I preach the gospel, I may make the gospel of Christ without charge, that I abuse not my power in the gospel. For though I be free from all men, yet have I made myself servant unto all, that I might gain the more.

Col 4:1-6

Masters, give unto your servants that which is just and equal; knowing that ye also have a Master in heaven. Continue in prayer, and watch in the same with thanksgiving; Withal praying also for us, that God would open unto us a door of utterance, to speak the mystery of Christ, for which I am also in bonds: That I may make it manifest, as I ought to speak. Walk in wisdom toward them that are without, redeeming the time. Let your speech be alway with grace, seasoned with salt, that ye may know how ye ought to answer every man.

Ps 119:66

Teach me good judgment and knowledge: for I have believed thy commandments.

CHAPTER 3

Getting Together

I already know that this is going to be one of the most read chapters in this book. For that reason I have to say that God is indeed faithful.

I truly believe that He calls men and women together in marriage and places us according to our predestined purpose. In my spiritual imagination it is almost as if when He put Adam to sleep and took his rib to make Eve He was simultaneously taking the rib of mankind and making an Eve for every one of them. I truly believe that was His intended perfect plan. Unfortunately they sinned, and with them all of us. As a result, Adams do not recognize Eves and Eves get confused about which Adam is theirs. Thankfully, there is a way back to the garden for the believer. It was there God said that it was not good for man to be alone. He also promises not to withhold any good thing from us. And it just so happens that a "wife" is considered a good thing. If you have a desire to be married you can rest assured that God has provided a mate. In my single days there was a couple that truly inspired me they are now pasturing a very blessed ministry in Michigan. One day the husband ministered to me and said, "Mary the fact that you desire a husband is your evidence that God has provided one for you". That statement changed me, and patience was born in heart. Submit to His timing, and let Him teach and instruct you in a way that will prepare you to walk in a happy and successful marriage.

I will share this story with you. There was one Christmas growing up like most American little girls I loved Barbie! This particular Christmas all I wanted was a Barbie Townhouse. I knew we didn't have much money so I had made sure to put my request in early enough for my mother to save up. Christmas was always special in our house and a time of year where we not only celebrated Christ's birth, but offered gifts to one another as well. My sister and I had these matching quilted slippered pajamas that zipped up the front and we were wearing them on this particular Christmas Eve. I remember feeling warm and toasty and not being able to fall asleep in anticipation of getting my townhouse. The next thing I knew my sister was waking me up and telling me it was Christmas, we ran into Mom's room and woke her up and darted to the tree. After having conducted a quick scan I could see there wasn't any package big enough to be my townhouse and started to feel a little disappointed but thought maybe I had miscalculated the size of the box. I opened one package after the other. First a new Barbie, then a Ken, then Barbie clothes, furniture, and the Barbie car, wow! My sister had gotten a bunch of Jamie Summers stuff, including the inflatable house. The funny thing is that even though I did not want Jamie Summers, I was beginning to covet that inflatable house. Just when I thought there were no more packages to open, my mother having quietly slipped away reappeared around the corner with a package asking, "What's this?" Instantly, I knew that was my townhouse and ran to attack it! I opened the package and sure enough, my mother who loved me had given me the Barbie townhouse. Now just think if she had not thought to give me all the accessories that I needed to go along with it, I would not really have been able to enjoy the full splendor of the house

What are you saying Mary? Well I am saying; let God give you everything you need to go along with the marriage you desire. Trust Him that each day of your singleness is a beautiful gift to prepare you for the family ahead of you. Now happily married, I can testify that God knows exactly what he is doing. I could not clearly see the gift of my singleness until I was well into my marriage. Marriage is a beautiful covenant and a blessing from God not to be mistaken for a fantasy.

I can testify that God is faithful because He prepared me, and then He gave me a man who is all the things I desired in this confession and much, much more.

Husband

Father, In Jesus name, I thank You that it is easy for me to rejoice with others because I know that I have not been forgotten. In Your name jealousy and loneliness are far from me because I believe that You will withhold no good thing from me and I know my husband is sent.

Thank You Lord that I have been made a wife and that he has been made a husband. I thank You that even before the set time for our marriage to be manifest the anointing of husband and wife is upon us, and it is made evident to others.

I thank You for my wonderful, Godly husband. I praise You that he is Your best. I am pleased with him because You have given him to me and I am confident that You know what I like and he is attractive to me. I thank You that he is a masculine man full of vitality and a born leader. I praise You that he is my head, and it is easy for me to submit to him according to Your word. Lord because You love me so much, You have given me a husband who is thoughtful and sensitive to my needs and who demonstrates care and affection for me in ways I can appreciate. Father I am happy that we enjoy one another and continue to develop similar interest. In the name of Jesus I rebuke impostors and look alikes set up by the enemy to deceive not only me but him also. I release my faith for the thee husband You have for me, in the name of Jesus. Father, I thank You that he sees me and knows who I am and that in Your name this confession is on his lips and You have given him the grace for me. I praise You that he always sees me as his wife, even while we are dating, and that he honors me and holds me in the highest esteem. I thank You that he finds me beautiful and Godly, and is pleased and never ashamed.

Thank You for his ministry and his place in Your kingdom. I praise You that because of his relationship with You he is guided by Your spirit and You consistently teach him to minister to me as a husband. In Your name and according to Your will he loves me as You love the church and just like You he is willing to die for me. God I praise Your name that You are first in my husband's life and he is a mature and seasoned believer who studies Your word and is diligent to apply it in his life.

I praise You father that our marriage is honorable to You and we have obtained favor of You Lord. In Your name and by Your anointing You are causing us to have dominion even now. I praise You that our marriage is a lighthouse for others, and that we are constantly seeking You to love better. In Your name our home is full of peace and the joy of You and one another. I thank You that we respect each other and whenever we disagree we seek to understand.

Thank You Lord that as iron sharpens iron, we are excellent stewards over Your money. I praise You that the principal of first fruits is operational in our marriage, and that as we give, fruit is multiplied back to us to be prosperous and have a super abundance that we may give and produce more in ministry, in business, and in our own lives. Thank You Father that we do not struggle but have a super-abundance according to the plentitude of Your storehouse.

Father I thank You that my husband is an excellent and loving father who exercises patience. I thank You that our family is important to him and he makes it a priority. Father I bless You for our children. I thank You for Your promises concerning them. I thank You that You have revealed yourself to them and they all have a heart for You. I thank You that they are not rebellious and full of folly. Thank You for their gifts of ministry and for protecting them from the traps of the enemy. I plead the blood of Jesus over their lives and everything concerning them. Thank You for using them to make Your name great in and through their lives.

Lord I love You and bless Your name. You are my first love and my complete God of everything. Thank You that as You fill my life with my mate and my family, my relationship with You only grows. Lord, You are always first and never forgotten or pushed aside.

In Your name I confess and believe

Scripture References

Isa 49:15

> Can a woman forget her sucking child, that she should not have compassion on the son of her womb? yea, they may forget, yet will I not forget thee.

Ps 84:11

> For the LORD God is a sun and shield: the LORD will give grace and glory: no good thing will he withhold from them that walk uprightly.

1Co 7:3

> Let the husband render unto the wife due benevolence: and likewise also the wife unto the husband.

Eph 5:23-25

> For the husband is the head of the wife, even as Christ is the head of the church: and he is the saviour of the body. Therefore as the church is subject unto Christ, so let the wives be to their own husbands in every thing. Husbands, love your wives, even as Christ also loved the church, and gave himself for it;

Pr 12:4

> A virtuous woman is a crown to her husband: but she that maketh ashamed is as rottenness in his bones

Pr 18:22

> Whoso findeth a wife findeth a good thing, and obtaineth favour of the LORD.

Ge 1:28

> And God blessed them, and God said unto them, Be fruitful, and multiply, and replenish the earth, and subdue it: and have dominion over the fish of the sea, and over the fowl of the air, and over every living thing that moveth upon the earth.

Ps 127:3-5

> Lo, children are an heritage of the LORD: and the fruit of the womb is his reward. As arrows are in the hand of a mighty man; so are children of the youth. Happy is the man that hath his quiver full of them: they shall not be ashamed, but they shall speak with the enemies in the gate.

CHAPTER 4

Getting the Family Blessed

You have heard it said that family is the basis of society. Well, I believe God has a purpose for the family as a unit as well, and when our entire families are operating in that God given purpose you just watch out! Can you imagine what would that be like? Does anybody know? Has anybody seen it? Just imagine an entire family, I am talking Daddy, Momma, Sister Girl, Brother Man, Aunties, Uncles, Cousins, and all the In-laws every one of them completely determined to live for God and operating in their purpose individually and collectively! What a force!

Well, I don't know about you but I certainly aspire to see it. I want my whole family saved, prosperous (according to the Bible's definition of prosperity), and when I say "whole" that includes the family into which I have married. I feel this thing very strongly down in my bones, and I pray for it and believe that it will manifest, and I know some members of my family are in faith with me. I just believe it ought to be the way God intended. That means I stand against divorce, disease, drugs, ignorance, complacency, isolation, jealousy, competition, gossip, meanness, early and accidental death, abortion, drunkenness, lust, fornication, evil communications, misunderstandings, lies, deceit, generational curses and a whole slew of other things that people just accept as part of life. It does not have to be so and I call it the way God said it!

With that in mind it is clear why everyday there are reports of families falling apart, or becoming the object of violence. The enemy knows if he can tear a family apart he has a good chance of keeping the members in personal chaos. Just today on the news I heard a story of two brothers getting into a fight and the one stabbed the other. I was so disturbed by the story because I believe brothers should work together and be willing to fight for one another, not against each other.

So many issues can be answered by simply understanding your lineage. Every time I visit the doctor I am asked questions about relative who are not even living anymore, simply because medical studies have shown huge correlations in family history to individual health. Since my own family has had a predisposition to certain illnesses I have been careful to not only confess the word of God over my life in those areas, but to also avoid certain behaviors that may increase risks. When I began to realize there were not only medical correlations but spiritual correlations as well once again I had to confess the word of God in my life and allow his blood to thoroughly cleanse my bloodline.

Even with the flaws and imperfections, just take a moment to think about your family and it's members. I am sure you are quite familiar with each one and their weaknesses. But if you could in this moment consider their strengths, you may be able to identify a recurring theme. God is completely intentional. No matter how "messed up" you may think your family to be. There is a reason you were born to this group of people and a reason God called them together as a family. I challenge you to try and discover that purpose, and even enlighten your other family members as to what you see.

In my own life I began to see that my maternal family was anointed with hospitality. They absolutely love to cook and throw a party and welcome strangers. They have many more callings, gifts, and talents individually. But as a unit when they come together for the purpose of hospitality they run like a very well oiled machine. They are always called upon to serve in the ministry of hospitality at conferences, councils, and concerts, etc. By doing this, they are building up the body of Christ with their spiritual gift as a family.

Ask God to open up your eyes so that you can see the same value and worth in your family that He sees and know His divine purpose in calling you together as a unit. As you confess the word of God over them may your family be restored!

Family

Father I thank You that our entire family is saved, delivered, and walking in righteousness. I praise Your name that the iniquities of the fathers will not be visited on the existing generations nor the generations to come because we repent of iniquity and have turned from sin. I confess that this is the generation of them that seek You and it is a chosen generation and royal priesthood. I praise You for the gifts and creativity that You have endowed to each member to be able to fulfill their purpose, and I thank You that we are not deceived by the enemy but know and believe the destiny You have for us.

I praise You that the fear and reverence of Your name is passed on in our family from generation to generation and Your mercy is upon us. I thank You for complete health in our family and rebuke sickness, disease, and early death in the name of Jesus. I thank You for long life and prosperity.

I thank You for happy, stable, committed marriages built on the foundation of Your word so that divorce and separation are far from us. I praise You that our family is supportive and produces healthy, loyal relationships and that others see the light of Christ in our lives witnessed by how we treat each other.

I thank You that we are good stewards over our time on this earth, and do not waste the gifts and talents entrusted to us because of fear and complacency but use them wisely to bless others. Lord, I thank You that we rejoice with those that rejoice because jealousy and competition are far from us.

Thank You for Your blessings and protection over our entire family, I praise you that your blood has purged our bloodline and any unclean thing has been washed and made new. I thank You that our purpose is fulfilled and the fruit of our labor is seen for generations to come.

Ps 78:6

That the generation to come might know them, even the children which should be born; who should arise and declare them to their children:

De 5:9

Thou shalt not bow down thyself unto them, nor serve them: for I the LORD thy God am a jealous God, visiting the iniquity of the fathers upon the children unto the third and fourth generation of them that hate me

Ps 24:6

This is the generation of them that seek him, that seek thy face, O Jacob. Selah.

Lu 1:50

And his mercy is on them that fear him from generation to generation.

1Pe 2:9

*But ye are a chosen generation, a royal priesthood, an holy nation, a peculiar * * people; that ye should shew forth the praises of him who hath called you out of darkness into his marvellous light:*

Jo 13:35

By this shall all men know that ye are my disciples, if ye have love one to another.

CHAPTER 5

Getting In Shape

This chapter is going to be short but not so sweet. I have to be honest and say that the area of health and fitness is currently one of my greatest challenges. I have done it all in the past to control weight you name it, I have tried it. More recently, however, the Lord has revealed to me that instead of trying to control my weight I should focus on being a good steward over my body. A good friend of mine once said, "You can loose weight on crack, but that doesn't mean it is good for you". Translation: There are lots of fad diets and gimmicks out there, but He has entrusted us with these vessels to use for His glory. That changes the ball game. If I am just trying to control weight then as long as I can fit in my clothes I have succeeded. On the contrary, if I am to be a good steward over this body I have to make sure that it is cared for properly and that it is working at its optimal level. This requires a strong and faithful commitment to balance overall health and nutrition. So I have been reading everything I can get my hands on, and asking God to give me wisdom to discern the truth.

Every little thing I learn has blessed my life and given me a greater understanding of how our bodies work and what we actually need. The greatest resource I have is my husband. He is a machine and absolutely loves physical fitness. So when I don't have the motivation to be physically active he is there inspiring me to get busy.

Another God-given gift to our health and well being is sleep. It came as a surprise to me the number of people who say they lay down at night but cannot sleep! I have heard personal accounts of individuals suffering from insomnia. They say things like "I feel like I should be doing something", or "My mind won't turn off", or "I just lay there and look at the ceiling". Many lack peace, which in turn affects their ability to sleep. When listening to these accounts, I am always reminded of Psalms 127:2 which says: "It is vain for you to rise up early, to sit up late, to eat the bread of sorrows: for so he giveth his beloved sleep."

Health and Fitness

Lord I thank You that I can do this. (Phil 4:13) I thank You for Your supernatural assistance in breaking every bondage and generational curse on my body, health, weight, and eating habits. I believe that since I have asked for Your help, I will be constantly convicted in the areas that I need to change, and will be motivated to excellence in the right exercise regime, diet, and overall health plan starting right now and lasting until I am in my glorified body.

I thank You that I strengthen my arms daily, and my children arise and call me blessed. Thank You that my youth is preserved and as the years pass my stature and stamina increase.

Thank You for the wisdom to discern the truth and the resources to understand this body that You have created. I thank You that vanity is far from me and my whole heart is turned to please You. I praise You that because Your yoke is easy and Your burden is light that this permanent change is anointed and accomplished with an ease I can only know in you. Thank You for Your divine help.

Php 4:13

I can do all things through Christ which strengtheneth me

1Co 6:19-20

Or don't you know that your body is the temple of the Holy Spirit, who lives in you and was given to you by God?

1Pe 2:24

Who his own self bare our sins in his own body on the tree, that we, being dead to sins, should live unto righteousness: by whose stripes ye were healed.

3Jo 1:2

Beloved, I wish above all things that thou mayest prosper and be in health, even as thy soul prospereth.

Pr 31:17

She girdeth her loins with strength, and strengtheneth her arms.

Pr 31:28

Her children arise up, and call her blessed; her husband also, and he praiseth her.

Isa 46:4

And even to your old age I am he; and even to hoar hairs will I carry you: I have made, and I will bear; even I will carry, and will deliver you.

Mt 11:30

For my yoke is easy, and my burden is light.

CHAPTER 6

Getting in His Presence

I cannot begin, in only one chapter, to do this topic justice. There are hundreds of books on worship, and thankfully all of the ones I have read offer some great insight. But I have more to say, and I believe God has blessed me with some wisdom and revelation to share His truths. I strongly believe that worship is a place built by choice, reserved in the heart of people who have decided that God is God and no matter what they will serve, honor, and love Him.

Having been Praise and Worship Director for over five years in the local assembly I can emphatically state that the church, in some cases, easily confuses the music with the worship, or with a strange idea that praise is upbeat and somehow worship is soft and delicate and must result in tears, to be powerful or even to be recognized as "real worship". The absolute worst misconception I have seen practiced is the one that says God "needs" worship. I have heard countless worship leaders say that very thing, and it makes me cringe every time I hear it because I am left with the question; "How can a God who simply speaks and it is so, have a need that He alone cannot meet? The answer is quiet simple, He does not need anything. So while He may love worship, it is clear that He is not an egotistically challenged God who needs our constant assurance that He is who He really is in order to be inspired.

No my brothers and sisters, He doesn't need it. But we do. We need to worship because having been made in His image we have the potential to become lifted up in pride and think that we are God. We may not want to admit it but it is in every single one of us. If you don't believe me find any two year old in any country and ask them who is running things.

Worship creates a permanent altar to God in our hearts. Worship sees God and recognizes that He is supreme. It says, I realize He has given me power and authority to subdue and have dominion, yet I will in no way shape or form attempt to elevate my person, needs, desires, creativity, influence, or anything He has given me in a way that would usurp His authority in my life.

That is indeed the heart of a true worshipper. Simply stated, the heart of a true worshipper is always submitted to God. When God sees that submission in our heart He can then trust us with the authority and dominion that He originally gave to Adam restoring that relationship and fellowship that we had with Him in the Garden before sin. That is why He loves worship.

There is no argument that music is one of the many powerful tools of worship. We sing praise to Him because of the permanent decision to elevate and Honor Him. And there are many times when the expression of worship through music will result in tears, or a joyful noise. But the dedication and authenticity of worship cannot be measured by those elements alone. Nor are they the only expressions or the goal of worship.

Now that we have discussed the heart of a true worshipper and explained that worship brings us back to the original state of mankind's relationship with God let's explore this a little further. The Bible says that God walked with Adam and Eve in the garden and they fellowshipped. That is exactly what worship does. It brings us into the presence of God in a way that restores fellowship and yes friendship.

I feel like I have just begun and I definitely do not want to stop this discussion on worship. However, I only have one chapter in this book to discuss worship and felt it necessary that we at least define worship for the purpose of understanding our corporate and personal faith confession.

During my tenure as Praise and Worship Director I was blessed to write a confession that began every session of corporate praise and worship and to my knowledge is still be used in the same way to this day. Every believer should not only understand worship but feel comfortable expressing their worship in music, money, service, conversation, and every other way we choose to honor God corporately and personally.

Worshippers

(Corporate)

Father We thank You, in response to Your Goodness,

We praise Your name because You have given us life and that more abundantly. With our hands we praise You, with our dance we celebrate You, with our song we adore You, with a shout we proclaim that You reign.

There is no situation, there is no circumstance, there is no enemy, and there is no foe that can prevent our praise, nor silence our worship. We worship You in spirit, We worship You in truth,

We are true worshippers.

Worshippers

(Personal)

Father I thank You that I may come boldly to Your throne of grace, I thank You for Your presence and the complete peace I have in You. I praise You for Your mighty acts in the entire world and in my life.

You have been consistent and true and I am overwhelmed by Your love. I bow my heart to You consistently, and thank You for the grace to be obedient against even my own will and desires. Father, I submit my entire being to You, and give You the gifts You have given me.

I worship You in spirit and in truth and I thank that my acts of worship are not tainted, performed for an audience, or the benefit of my own esteem, but to honor and esteem You alone.

Father, in Your presence I am humbled by Your greatness, and the greatness You have called me to. You are always my King, my Lord, and my All.

Ps 107:8

Oh that men would praise the LORD for his goodness, and for his wonderful works to the children of men!

Job 10:10

The thief cometh not, but for to steal, and to kill, and to destroy: I am come that they might have life, and that they might have it more abundantly.

Ps 149:1-3

Praise ye the LORD. Sing unto the LORD a new song, and his praise in the congregation of saints. Let Israel rejoice in him that made him: let the children of Zion be joyful in their King. Let them praise his name in the dance: let them sing praises unto him with the timbrel and harp

Ps 146:10

The LORD shall reign for ever, even thy God, O Zion, unto all generations. Praise ye the LORD.

Job 4:23 -24

But the hour cometh, and now is, when the true worshippers shall worship the Father in spirit and in truth: for the Father seeketh such to worship him.God is a Spirit: and they that worship him must worship him in spirit and in truth.

CHAPTER 7

Getting out of Debt

Something happens in worship. You can hear God clearly and you know He has work for you to do. I believe that debt is one of Satan's devices used to prevent God's people from having a real impact and fulfilling their purposes. Say what you want, but money does answer all things. Now God can bless us with favor to get money or the value of what money would offer. But if your credit is so awful that you can't muster up the courage to walk into a bank or your lifestyle is such that you can't be trusted with favor, we have a problem.

Financial stewardship is another topic I cannot cover in one chapter it is way too vast. But I will address the basics. In my opinion, our stewardship of money is closely linked to worship. True worshippers are under a conviction to be good stewards plain and simple. Remember, the heart of a worshipper knows it has been entrusted with dominion but answers to God. So I can't believe you if you say you are a true worshipper because you are on the praise team, and the lifestyle does not match. You must bring forth the fruit of a true worshipper.

Before we can talk about money, let me be very clear. There is no faith confession, debt counseling, or advice I can give that will help your situation if you are not tithing. Bottom line, it is not optional and you will produce nothing but "lack" if you think you can have a financial plan that does not include bringing at least a 10th of all into the Kingdom of God. This does not happen after you pay the rent it happens right off the top just like good ole' Uncle Sam and by the way it is a 10th of the gross in case you were wondering. That just gets you operating in obedience. If you want to operate in obedience and blessing you better pop an offering on top of that. Trust me, you can give your way out of debt!

Having said all of that, now we can talk. There is good debt, and there is bad debt. In this chapter we are talking about bad debt. Money borrowed to purchase an asset that will appreciate, such as a home, or equipment used for a business is a good investment because handled correctly the money you borrowed will not outlive the potential value of the asset or

what it may produce. However, if you borrow to purchase items such as furniture, clothing, etc., simply because you don't have the discipline to save up for those kinds of things, it is a very bad investment. Those items depreciate rapidly and the principal and interest you will pay for them no longer supports their value and you have created a bad debt. Eventually you will have less money than what you need because you are paying current income for old debts that no longer have any value, while at the same time incurring new debts for things that in the future will have little to no value. This cycle will lead a person further and further into debt.

In plain English,. Stop going to the mall charging clothes, and financing furniture, and spending more money than what you make. Live within your means, and create a budget that pays tithes and offerings, and includes a savings plan to pay off old debts and finance new purchases.

Well, those are the basics; let's get our faith working in the right direction.

Stewardship

Lord I thank You that because I bring the first fruits of all I have into the storehouse that the blessing of a tither is upon me and I am anointed with creativity, favor, opportunity, and the power to get wealth.

I praise You that I am a good steward and a sower and You can trust me with multiplied seed. I praise You that stinginess, and selfishness is far from me, and I not only bring an offering but am filled with compassion to care for the widow, the fatherless, and the stranger

I thank You that there are not holes in my bags and there is always a super abundance to give into the Kingdom, provide for the needs of my home, business, and others. I am pleased to be the lender and not the borrower and I thank You for the wisdom of good stewardship.

Father I stand against compulsive buying and poverty, and I thank You for wisdom to buy houses and lands, and for the discipline to save an inheritance to pass on not only to my children but to my children's children as well.

I thank You that the devourer has been rebuked, and I am prosperous and that all of my accounts are overflowing. I praise You that any reports reflect my credibility and the character of my good name.

I thank You that You continue to provide instruction, education, and knowledge leading me in the paths of wisdom and my understanding is increased. Thank You for the resources and outlets that are opening up my mind and transforming my thinking.

Father I thank You for the things that You have prepared, I receive my inheritance and the blessing of Abraham is on me in Jesus name.

Mal 3:10-12

Bring ye all the tithes into the storehouse, that there may be meat in mine house, and prove me now herewith, saith the LORD of hosts, if I will not open you the windows of heaven, and pour you out a blessing, that there shall not be room enough to receive it. And I will rebuke the devourer for your sakes, and he shall not destroy the fruits of your ground; neither shall your vine cast her fruit before the time in the field, saith the LORD of hosts. And all nations shall call you blessed: for ye shall be a delightsome land, saith the LORD of hosts.

Le 27:30

And all the tithe of the land, whether of the seed of the land, or of the fruit of the tree, is the LORD'S: it is holy unto the LORD.

De 14:22

Thou shalt truly tithe all the increase of thy seed, that the field bringeth forth year by year.

Ex 23:19

The first of the firstfruits of thy land thou shalt bring into the house of the LORD thy God. Thou shalt not seethe a kid in his mother's milk.

Pr 3:9

Honour the LORD with thy substance, and with the firstfruits of all thine increase:

2Co 9:10

Now he that ministereth seed to the sower both minister bread for your food, and multiply your seed sown, and increase the fruits of your righteousness;

De 24:19

When thou cuttest down thine harvest in thy field, and hast forgot a sheaf in the field, thou shalt not go again to fetch it: it shall be for the stranger, for the fatherless, and for the widow: that the LORD thy God may bless thee in all the work of thine hands

Hag 1:6

Ye have sown much, and bring in little; ye eat, but ye have not enough; ye drink, but ye are not filled with drink; ye clothe you, but there is none warm; and he that earneth wages earneth wages to put it into a bag with holes.

Pr 22:7

The rich ruleth over the poor, and the borrower is servant to the lender.

Pr 31:16

She considereth a field, and buyeth it: with the fruit of her hands she planteth a vineyard.

Pr 13:22

A good man leaveth an inheritance to his children's children: and the wealth of the sinner is laid up for the just

Pr 13:18

Poverty and shame shall be to him that refuseth instruction: but he that regardeth reproof shall be honoured.

Ge 12:2-3

And I will make of thee a great nation, and I will bless thee, and make thy name great; and thou shalt be a blessing: And I will bless them that bless thee, and curse him that curseth thee: and in thee shall all families of the earth be blessed.

Ge 28:3-4

And God Almighty bless thee, and make thee fruitful, and multiply thee, that thou mayest be a multitude of people; And give thee the blessing of Abraham, to thee, and to thy seed with thee; that thou mayest inherit the land wherein thou art a stranger, which God gave unto Abraham

Lu 6:38

Give, and it shall be given unto you; good measure, pressed down, and shaken together, and running over, shall men give into your bosom. For with the same measure that ye mete withal it shall be measured to you again.

NOTES

Mary Tiller-Woods resides in Nashville, TN with her husband and is an accomplished recording artist and songwriter. "Her keep it simple, and keep it real" style of writing is refreshing and insightful. Couple that style with her keen biblical perspective and you have what promises to be a long-time favorite that serves to enhance the believer's confession of faith for generations to come.

www.ingramcontent.com/pod-product-compliance
Lightning Source LLC
Chambersburg PA
CBHW031530040426
42445CB00009B/469